Eyes *of the* Heart,
Glimpses of the Holy

JANET SMITH POST

Eyes of the Heart
© 2022 by Janet Post. All rights reserved.

No part of this book may be reproduced in any written, electronic, recording, or photocopying form without written permission of the publisher or author. The exception would be in the case of brief quotations where permission is specifically granted by the publisher or author.
www.JanetSmithPost.com

Editor: Susan Carter
Cover photo: Dick Vogel
Book and Cover Design: Rebecca Finkel, F+P Graphic Design

ISBN trade paper: 9780578342290

First Edition
Printed in the USA

For Eleanor, The Lady of the Light

and for my son,
Joshua, who made the writing
of this book possible.

" . . . the eyes of your heart being enlightened,
that you may know . . ."
—Ephesians 1:18

Contents

Such was His Power 11
In Another Time 12
It's a Good Thing, God 13
Spring Time 15
Deserted House 16
"Per-spec-tive," said the Whirlwind 17
Master Mimes 19
Svetyskhoveli Cathedral 20
I Knock 21
The Alpha and Omega 22
Little Boy 23
Spruce Up! 25
Lullaby to Baby Jesus 26
First Visit to the Sea 28
Cerebral Catastasis 30
God's Turn 31
Anchorite Apprentice 33
Great Blue Heron 34
Our Unseen God 36
Monument Valley 37
Silent Glissandos 39
Look! See! 40
It is Finished 41
The Button Tin 43
Trace of Mercy 46
Can It Be? 48

Divine Design	50
Rumi's Field	52
If	54
Reconciliation	55
Planting Seeds	56
Blackberry Grit	57
Changing of the Guard	59
Confirmation in the Laundry Room	61
Burnt by Branta	63
Earliest Light	65
The Cipher Tree	66
When	68
I've Gone Hunting for my Goat	69
Scarlet Manna	72
Beloved	73
For Larry	74
Circumcision of the Heart	76
The Eternal Mystery	78
Eyes of the Heart	81

At night,
the
soul upon the pillow,
empty chalice
waiting.

The Beloved
brings a golden thought,
a surprise
kiss
upon
the
mind.

Such was His Power

And the angels gathered
to sing the Overture of Creation.
A word from His mouth
and the earth rolled out of nothing
to find its path
through the vast fields of space.
With His power,
He poured the oceans to their brim,
hung up the skies to dry,
and filled every mountain,
stream and cranny,
with moving, rollicking life.

And yet, and yet,
This same Power allowed Himself
to be taken up by the Holy Spirit,
to be reduced to less
than could be seen in a thimble,
to be planted in the dark womb of a peasant girl.

And yet, and yet...
we are all peasant girls,
birthing Him anew!

In Another Time

In another time,
at the sound of celestial decree,
the emptying began.
The angels turned away
to hide their faces,
as He departed
from oceans of light
and a thousand, thousand adorations.
He descended,
dropping gowns of glory,
until
stripped to clay,
He walked among us.

Yet, as truth cannot be hidden,
the heaven of Him
pierced through the clay
with clarity of diamonds,
which also come
from another time.

It's a Good Thing, God

It' a good thing, God
that no one knows your name.
The secret vowels were lost
in the Hebrew mist,
and the consonants are not telling.

If we found your name today,
we'd enact further divisions,
plant flags of precise enunciation
and rightful ownership,
Eventually, we'd profane Your name
like every *gosh* and *golly*.

Adjectives and nouns are nearly
all we have,
to dust Your fingerprints:
for all things wear the garments of God,
as every poet knows.

Verbs are less reliable,
though they once were certain:
In the beginning God *created*...
But they've been overused.
We recite God's *will* to case in point
like lawyers in a fray.
So, it's best we do not know your name.

It unites us in our ignorance.
You are wise to conceal...
You are the God who hides,
found only with the heart's eyes,
unless a beast[1] should enter there
 to blind the light,
or a Claudius[2] pour poison into the ear.

---

[1]John Cassian: an early monk who taught that one should trace out the footsteps of whatever enters into the chambers of the heart, lest haply some beast enter there.

[2]Shakespeare: *The Tragedy of Hamlet*

Spring Time

The old sand cherry bush, barren of leaves,
stripped by age of winter
is now laid low by late spring snow—
wet, heavy on each branch.
Its thin arms downcast with burden
nearly to the ground.

I passed the window more than once
saw its sadness there,
imprisonment
beneath the hold of snow.
sentenced to wait the weight.

Nothing to do but boot-up, wade out
set it right, and shake away the snow.
What I hadn't thought to feel,
was its nearly human push, its force of leap
from bowed-down limb, to right itself again,
and could it speak, each limb would sing
"Ye-s-s-s-s-s," to its trace of arc,
the whole curved way.

Will this then be, our final day,
when the body's hold is cleared away,
and the Spirit springs—no soars—to right
and sings its zing, like an arrow shot.

Deserted House

The roads cross and divide here,
and just over there—unnoticed—is the house,
that now slants on all sides, but mostly backward,
like the past, that held the life of Seola,
who looked at us, when she came to town,
from behind dark eyes, that knew not to speak.

There, in that forgotten furrow, stands the plow,
where her husband's hand once gripped,
the rusted curve of handle, and plowed the earth,
where Seola scattered hopeful seeds,
then bent, slender as a stem, over the rows
to harvest food to set before their hunger,
at the table, where we were careful not to sit.
Alone in her woman's life, like that purple coneflower
there on the margin of the goldenrods.

"Per-spec-tive," said the Whirlwind

This ball of earth is knee-deep-to-God in spectacular!
Take those big horned sheep—
who stand on the side of a rock-face wall
at near-ninety degrees—
nonchalant and chewing free grass.

Where a thousand silver streams
slide fearless over cliffs
rappelling free of any ropes.
They free-fall down the canyon walls.

On faraway Savannas, the elephant,
 unintentional Kingdom Mother,
her largeness clears a path so
little creatures find their way,
digs wells with her tusk in dried
 riverbeds, and everybody drinks.
Rain returns to fill her elephant tracks,
sweet little pools for tadpoles.

Far up on a granite spire
in a teaspoon soil of pot
a single flower blooms.
It never seeks a vase,
content to nod its head
only to the passing wind.

On deepest unseen ocean floors
where sunlight never goes,
whole communities celebrate.
They sway away in the watery dark
and sip from lips of thermal vents.

In the midst of all your importance
and urgent days of harried cares,
Consider this:
Somewhere, a whole of whale is
is standing on its tail,
leaping up for simple joy-of-leap,
and two miles down in a diamond mine
a nematode is worming.
Hot, and dry and short on air
it's slithering right along!
We're all just specks of the spectacular.
Per-spec-tive, that's the thing!
So, live as *per* your *speck!*

Master Mimes

Consider the sparrow,
small and drab,
in every common place.
It has no weapon against hawk or owl.
Yet, fearless on the open branch,
it sings full-throated, with confidence of a king.

Consider the lily,
rising from deep darkness of earth,
risking one green finger to seek the light.
Naked, yet believing, it follows longing upward,
until, at last, clothed in unseen gown,
it opens every petal wide,
surprising and surpassing
the Satin-Silks of Solomon.

Svetyskhoveli Cathedral

(Upon hearing Iraqi and Syrian refugees singing at the Svetyskhoveli Cathedral in Mtskheta, Georgia.)

The heavy drone begins,
a haunting to startle the sleeping ear.
Now begins a wail above the drone,
a mournful longing,
pitched above the weary way,
stretched ageless.

It strikes our sympathetic scars,
which shudder—resonate.
It pierces through till we confess,
 "Yes, we know this primal song,"
the one we silence with our illusions.

We, too, are tethered here,
round and round this ring of earth,
turning on its dirge through seamless time.
These ancient Aramaic strains remind
the world is mostly sorrow, not a stage.

And yet, and yet,
these—who journeyed, fresh from war,
with nothing left to carry but each other,
lift up, lift up, to keen the shapes and sounds of God!

I Knock

I am the door
through which your door opens.

I am the calling
to your hiding behind.

I am the voice that
finds your hearing.

I invite my chair beside your hearth

Put aside your shame of lack,
Do not fear on what we'll dine,
I am the bread
and I am the wine.

The Alpha and Omega

Our past and present times
are not marks upon Your wall.
You wear no pocket watch, no dial of sun
You live all eternal ticks as one.
You see a man and see him whole.

You pass the man fully grown,
"Is not this not he who sat and begged?"
 they ask.
You see him embryo in the womb,
You see his tissues as they wrongly form,
as You see his healing sight restored,
No disjointed lapse of time for Your
End from the Beginning.

Our name for him is "the man born blind."
What is your name for a man
seen whole by Your Eternal eyes?

Little Boy

Little boy at his desk,
 His sleeves hang
on his small, round shoulders,
which have not grown enough
to shoulder.

Little boy-bloom,
droops as on a curved stem,
staring down at its roots.
I cannot see his face,
 the stain of purple-blue,
savaged on his velvet cheek,
beside his swollen eye.

The memo on my teacher's desk informs:
"Officials will arrive."
"Do not permit his father."

I recite the rules; the lessons chant,
 and all the words point their fingers
 with echoed, forkéd tongues.

"I pledge allegiance to the flag,
With liberty and justice for all.
The sticks are crooked, seven eight.
How can we lay them straight?"

"A long "a" sound is found in *fāce*.
A short "a" is found in *săd*.
The deepest "a" sinks in the throat,
like a moan, and sounds like *Fäther*."

"*Childhood* contains two syllables.
There's only one in *life*.
Trust means to feel safe,
and *safe* ends with a silent "e,"
as does the word, *hope*, which also
ends, silently."

Spruce Up!

Spruce up!
The Lord is coming to bear us aloft...
Wouldn't want to be
Lookin' frowzy in the faith
When He lifts us up for a look see!

Lullaby to Baby Jesus
(In Black Spiritual tradition)

Little Baby Jesus,
What'd you come down here for?

Can't lay your head in a King's bed now,
Cattle and sheep and a hay bed now,
Come down here to be a poor boy now.
Little Baby Jesus, what'd you come down here for?

Swaddling clothes for a royal coat,
Trade your throne for a fisherman's boat
Livin' out words that the prophets wrote.
Little Baby Jesus, what'd you come down here for?

Hung up the moon and stars with your hand,
Now you're gonna be a carpenter man,
Tellin' all the folks 'bout a Promise Land,
Little Baby Jesus, what'd you come down here for?

Can't take a walk on a golden street,
Sandals and dust for your weary feet,
Bringin' us love so free and sweet,
Little Baby Jesus, what'd you come down here for?

Come down here to do some laughin' with us,
Come down here to do some cryin' with us,
Come down here to do some dyin for us!
Little Baby Jesus, Little Baby Jesus!

First Visit to the Sea

My daughter lived
in a saltbox house, near the sea.
She packed us a lunch, a lovely
basket with a thermos of tea—
nicer than she was raised.
We climbed the berm and there
Kierkegaard's God moment
that arrives, "light with the step of sudden."
The ground I had known—first and only—ceased.
Water, water, vast, undulating water.
No hills, or forests, or curves in the road,
nothing between me and the furthest horizon of blue,
stretching far beyond conclusion, like eternity.
The amniotic fluid of all births,
now azure, now cerulean,
now breaking white, wave on wave,
sweeping in to sleek the sand,
then drawing back and sweeping in again,
compelled by ancient knowing.

In time, we sat on the low, stone wall.
My daughter spread a cloth and lunch.
I tried to say a simple grace—
thank God for the food,
and this new wonder I sought to greet.
But when a great thing swells the heart
and in turn, the throat,
the press permits no words,
only tears know the way,
like salty remnants of the sea,
they fell in recognition.

Cerebral Catastasis

A thought is born
In darkest cell,
and holds its tongue
and waits to tell.

Yet sends a shaft—
the slightest ray,
down virgin path,
of guarded gray,
Till conscience bids
its fearless sleuth
to bring the mind
to see the truth—

Nay, drags the mind
in wanting dread,
as children seek,
ghost tales at bed.

The mind thus caught
cannot escape,
the growing light
of nearly said.
which turns full-glare
to state its name
and nothing more
remains the same.

God's Turn

Mine a waking-habit of the night,
A time to pray,
requests neglected in the day.

But first,
careful to bring my offerings,
my adjectival phrases,
to craft my similes,
to plagiarize Your scriptures,
with words called *praise* and *worship*.
A one-sided conversation,
I bring to You.
I do the climbing upward,
I sing my love song
to Your vacant balcony.

Till this night, with no warning,
You appear!
Like all things sudden, shock is!
You descend all around in light-filled vastness,
Space and Presence
Faceless and Absolute:
The Great I Am!
I am discovered, huddled,
scant and wordless,

no Moses rock, cleft for me.
I've rung the castle bell
and here stands the King!

As Your unexpected coming,
So is Your vanishing,
leaving only sweetness,
a nearly playful game
I didn't know to play.
And I am left
with infant's "peek-a-boo!"
My soul, wide with
child's expectant hope
to have You peek once more!

ANCHORITE APPRENTICE
A Sonnet to the Bridegroom

Hope is the hallowed hold of the heart, there
where that which can be seen, cannot reside,
just that which evidence cannot provide,
stored in the heart's womb on sinews that bear,
longings yearned taut and strained time-thin with wear,
conceived in faith, when all strength is denied,
waiting to birth understanding supplied,
pleadings breathed to air and distilled in prayer.

Then comes the way of betrayal's dark night,
vultures of doubt feed on hopes one by one.
The heart in despair now falls from the light,
but the anchor still stays by unknown strung.
The heart traces blind braille to tethering's might,
Found tied to Him—by Him—already done.

Great Blue Heron

She first caught sight of him,
leaving his sleep in the reeds,
deep-beating wing strokes of lift,
then spreading wide, wings like arms.
Intersecting mid-wings, fore and aft,
his very long and supple neck, now
straight as if it turned to wood,
length of legs, extended line behind.
His shadow formed upon the ground,
as though the sky had drawn a cross.

Sometimes she saw him, head held high
tranquil, tall, and still as a rock.
"Symbol of Peace," she had read,
and "A Messenger of God."
Yet some strange dread clung round
 his oval lobe of body, feathers
the only armor for his heart,
as if he were a Christ bird in disguise.

At times, he bent his hinged knee back—
opposite from humans—then lifted foot
so placed with care; stepping as if to
test uncertain ground; then statue-stood,
on legs, thin and tall as stalks of reed.

Face set like flint beneath blue crown
with golden eye of keenest sight.
Feathers, pale of blue and gray,
and apron plume like Tzitzit fringe,
his long neck bent, as though to pray.

Now it was night, and moonlight
with push of waves across the lake
spread a silver road, uphill, uphill,
to light a silver king,
fixed in a silver tree,
motionless, alone,
like the moon.

Two shadows on the balcony,
their manner made her know, they
were waiting 'til she passed.
And then, their bullet with its hiss,
sliced through the hide of dark,
as hate with hate must find its mark:
the silver light, with its silver cry.

Our Unseen God

We cannot see our God, today.
He is not carved from Dagon's mold,
to fall upon his face,
and leave his hands in the open door,
where men once leapt
the threshold in his honor.

We do not see or hold an arrow
silver-made, like Diana's bow,
cast from the same molten pot
that fashions coins for merchandise.

Nor do we bring Him cakes
like crescent moons,
as others laid on Athens's altars.

No, in this time of waiting earth,
God is seen by braille of human heart,
where love lights the heart-eyes
to read his splendid words,
and faith, alone the lens,
unveils his being there.

Monument Valley

Red sand, traveled grain by grain,
down primordial creases of time,
migrants from distant ancestral Rockies,
carried on water and wind,
salted here, layer on layer baked by desert sun,
vast sandstone plinth
stretched far beyond horizons.

Then relentless chiseling by wind's router,
dervish dances of feral waters
swirling patterns, sculpting galleries
terra cotta spires,
pillars to throne the rule of cougars,
buttes to warm the diamond backs
of snakes and eggs of cactus wrens,
a thousand, thousand fissures to
crevice horned toads and whiptail lizards,
distant, ribboned mesas to cradle sunsets
red as fire wheel flowers.

Into this primal land rides "The Duke,"
cameras rolling, astride the manicured horse,
stunt-man saddled. Filming crew staged
on thrown-down, wooden pallets,
work to mimic authenticity.

Soundman holds jib arm overhead,
recording scripted words for silver screen,
illusion for the eyes.
I, a modern tourist, listen to the guide:
"Twelve John Wayne movies filmed here."

Driving home, I receive no fanfare
from rust-red desert floor, no curtain drawn
by purpled sage or fuchsia cactus bloom,
no rustled excitement through the rabbit brush,
no whistle from the yucca spears.
In *media res,* the movie begins—silent film projected
on small screen window of my car,
backlit by the crimson sun. I see the distant
Navajo boy, galloping there,
silent drumming hooves of painted pinto
seen between flash-fast frames of junipers and pinons,
knees and legs pressed tight to
bare flanks of pony.
Free joyous wild-boy rides
with ancient Anasazi blood,
 long hair streaming, wind-swept,
black as jib-arm of raven, flying just above.

The wind whispers with rhythm of tires,
"One ticket to this view,"
"God's impromptu—just for you."

Silent Glissandos

Mortals live with savage sorrows
and joys that flood to furthest edge.
So, they need the gift of tears.

God fashioned tiny furrows,
threaded to cornered eyes,
leading up to unseen basins,
where all the futures wait.

And there are sacred moments,
when a solemn thing swells the heart,
and, in turn, the throat. The press permits
no words. Only tears know the way.
So, humans need these silent sounds
that they might *hear* another's face.

And, if tears are not vainly practiced,
but flow unsummoned from the heart,
they mean that one has stepped upon a truth,
and drops, reflecting purest light,
fall as holy fonts, to baptize a sacred face.

Look! See!
(In honor of Rumi)

Look! See!
The night sky is wearing all its diamonds.
The moon has silvered the roses
along the garden wall.

There are love rings on every finger of your hand,
and the silken gown of joy
kisses your ankles.

Follow the Beloved to
the sound of dancing
and the
carillon of bells
twirling in your heart.

It is Finished

"It is finished," Christ said,
and sat down, at
the right hand of God.
The angels, who are watchers,
looked out to see
what mortals would do
with this paid-in-full decree.

They saw old ones, stooped
like mothers over cradles,
nursing memories of sins,
strapped like phylacteries
to their ancient backs.

They saw young men and maidens,
seeking shadows, stepping from the light,
like children stepping over cracks,
believing the foolish game that
what is bargained has no consequence.

They saw the bitter ones,
clutching claim checks of revenge,
swallowing home-brewed poisons
between clenched teeth.

They saw those pardoning their neighbors,
with their right hand, and with the left,
 receiving secret pride.
taking bows for the blood of Christ.

But from time to time
along the practiced paths of hiding,
the angels saw those who
encountered the eye of God.

The grace of His gaze,
saw to the roots of their fig-leaf lies
and they knelt, naked-deep in forgiveness,
free to rise in grateful exposure of the light.

The Button Tin

My mother saved buttons in a round red tin,
a red as definite as blood.
As a girl I used to wade my fingers
through the pool of buttons,
up to my finger-thighs.
Then like Moses, I'd rake a path,
part the sea, send buttons
colliding to fill the wake,
a wonderful clattering sound,
feeding on its own confusion,
clacking machine-gun staccatos
against tin walls.

My mother sat nearby, sewing
in patient, unwavering peace,
and would not be baited
by my childish stridulating.

A foreigner lodged within
the button tin, a bullet:
a .30 caliber, unspent shell,
Uncle Leonard's souvenir from the war,
dropped one day among the buttons.
As in any land, time and
occupancy gave a title deed,
and there it stayed.

The other un-button was
my mother's thimble, a finger helmet,
worn to prevent the shedding of blood.
I wear it now on my woman's finger.

My turn to sew buttons,
on the right for daughters,
on the left for sons,
a warrior's way conferred,
knights unbuttoning jackets
with the left,
 to draw swords swiftly
 with the right,
defending rights that time,
or might decreed.

My children rake their fingers,
through the button sea,
Unlike my mother, I yell protest.
I asked her how she never raised her voice.
"I never cared enough to yell," she says.
Uncle Leonard retorts, "That's easy said,
behind shut doors on cushioned
sewing chairs. There's things in war
could make a dead man scream."

The bullet still remains among the buttons,
its place changing with each strafe of fingers.
The line between too much caring
or caring not enough, still unmarked,
in the shifting cacophony of circumstance.

The Trace of Mercy

Unlikely words can share their roots:
the old French sprout of *wound*
is the very stem of *blessing*,
and the aged English child of
bless was birthed from *blood*.

The ancients traced the vine
of scars to blossoms red.
It twined their tongues
to branch the root
and make of one word, two.

There are countless gifts
from countless wounds,
here are but a few:

The wound of abandonment
bears the blessing of attachment,
tight as a leaf pressed within the bud
to fully open, only when all the petals do,
and stays until the last to fall.

The wound of rejection,
anoints the expectations,
refines the hope to wait
for greater certainties.

The laceration of pride
bestows its absolution,
allows the healing walk
from the stage of borrowed fame
to find its sweetest place
in the true number of its row.

All wounds and blessings
learn their worth
by sound of wood and nails,
and Old Latin *merces*,
and Anglo-French *merci*,
bestow their thanks for mercy**
paid by price of endless blood.

Round the wound that's raw and bare,
mercy's finger wills the trace,
to find the blessing hidden there.

Blessure: The Old French words for *wound* and *blessing* share the same root.

**Mercy* (Middle English, from Anglo-French merci, from Medieval Latin merced-, merces, from Latin, "price paid, wages", from merc-, merxi "merchandise") is benevolence, forgiveness, and kindness in a variety of ethical, religious, social, and legal contexts.

Can It Be?

Can it be, Oh God,
that you have need of me?
Like the fish who carried a coin.
A common tilapia earning its
name: *St. Peter's fish?*
Do you have need of a trinket from me?
I who breathe each breath
from breath of You.

Can it be, O God,
that you have need of me?
Like the colt who waited at its
mother's side, till these spoken words:
"The Lord has need of it."
The colt who carried the weight
of God's beloved son.
And I, who cast my daily weight on You?

Can it be, O God,
that you have need of me?
Like Spikenard that grew to give
itself in the crush of oil
to bathe Your feet?
And I, who gave nothing
for Your death, but sin?

Can it be? Can it be?
Then let me be a fish
to carry a trinket for the tax,
or the Spikenard crushed
and poured from alabaster jar.
Whatever the purpose,
that I should be the one,
I wait, like the colt at its post
until I hear, "The Lord has need of you."

Divine Design

You dwell also in our *future*, Beloved,
there beyond our knowing,
a door that *only* opens tick-by-tick.
Sometimes, You drop bread crumbs
from the other side…a kind of game,
like sending Peter and John to the village,
to the first man that they meet,
"He'll carry a pitcher of water,"
You say—then send them away.
But did You instruct the water guy?
(This game makes us nervous. We lose control.)
Calculate distance and speed of each step,
two opposites—approaching.
When was the pitcher filled up with water?
The "what ifs" increase—exponentially!
What if John stops, to offer a greeting?
Or Peter sits down, shaking sand from his shoe?
Or the water guy talks too long at the well?

"Follow the man till he enters a house,
and when you're inside, seek the owner."
The *owner?* Another coordinate!
We're counting jelly beans deep in the jar!
"Tell him, the teacher has need of a room."

This game has no logic
on our side of the door.
No linear means!
It's illusive, improbable—
like Your beginning—which has no end,
and Your end—which has no beginning.

You played this same game,
with the donkey, tied to its colt,
and the fish with its coin for the tax.
Shall we think of Your bread crumbs
when our way grows dark
or the chances thin, till there's no way to win?
Do we fret and fright through labyrinth walls,
worry and stress till we wilt and we fall?

Or was it a game after all?
Or a ray of light from beyond the door,
to share a glimpse of Divine Design?
So come, come!
Dance and sing,
swing the fish round on a golden string,
ride the donkey to a hidden room,
where palms are spread and the water is wine,
where the tax is all paid,
and the Bridegroom reigns.

Rumi's Field

Out beyond ideas of wrong doing and right doing, there is a field.
I'll meet you there.

—Mewlana Jalaluddin Rumi,
Wondrous Birds Grow from the Palm of My Hand

I didn't cry the day
the planes flew through walls
and the towers fell,
the day the T.V. cameras saw
what took our eyes,
so
long
to
believe.

I didn't cry the day,
we dropped rich death bombs on
ragged, beggar mountains,
or the day,
I saw the old man in Afghanistan—or maybe
he was a fireman in New York—
arms burnt black,
staring in silence from white gauze bandages,
never looking down at his
leg that wasn't
there.

My anguish was
too great to know its name
and could not cry,
until the day I saw
the field
we did not find:
the day
we dropped food
like manna from the sky,
and the little child sat
in the doorway
eating raisins from our bag,
and we remembered one another's
sweetness under the sun.

If

If your heart is a grave,
like the ground beneath your house,
lost to the sunlight,
and the bloom of the rose,
and the foot of the robin,
where nothing grows,
but the spider's web,
and foreboding creeps,
on insect feet,
across the lifeless soil,
then,
throw open the lid of your casket-soul,
let the raindrops,
kiss your wakened face
feel fresh wind upon your cheeks.
Rise up,
fill your hair with pearls,
put on a fresh gown of turning around,
for the Beloved waits in the garden,
and He is restless for your returning.

Reconciliation

The Scalene Triangle is unequal on all its sides;
Abraham, Sarah, and Hagar
were such a cornered three.
Hagar, despised in Sarah's eyes,
Sarah's hope, barren as her womb,
and Abraham, mate to both,
binding the triangled-two.

In time, Isaac was added to Ishmael.
The two young boys—escaping
the slant of their tents—ran free,
straight to the sunshine of play.

Yet scorn will find its punishment
and Sarah, spying the boys cried out:
"The son of Hagar, shall not be co-heir!"
 And Abraham, in unfathomed grief,
sent Ishmael—firstborn son—away.
Apologists are quick to say
this was God's plan—true for that day,
But a higher Light was yet to shine,
and the boys—now men—found a ray
in the mourn of Abraham's death.
Of the reconciliation
only this is told: Isaac and Ishmael,
bearing the weight of their father,
buried him that day.

Planting Seeds

In the soft, turned earth
I scatter seeds so small, the country folk would
wink their name: "no see ums."
How can a speck—size of my needle's point—
hold God's whole plan for its life?

Some sprout to birth a narrow green,
thin as the thread from my spool;
others birth a miniature green bow-tie—
perfect fit for the spider near-by.
Following hidden messages,
they fashion foliage,
'til they reach their fragrant crowns,
each a chosen color from its code.

Can we not, then, trust this Secret Plan,
the still small voice, whispering the way,
that insists to send a tap root down,
to hold against the storm,
believe the unfolding of the mystery—
 to branch us leaf-on-leaf,
urging us each day, the cutting free of tillers,
that we might come to fully blossom,
with hearts that open
soft as a petal's skin.

Blackberry Grit

It wasn't the work of picking the blackberries,
harvesting a thousand knobby, oval beads,
or washing them one by one to lay
in freezer's winter grave, to be harvested anew,
and some to gather but a day
beneath a baking crust of Autumn brown.
Nor was it the Ozark sun of morning,
reaping dew from the maidenhair ferns,
nor even the sacredness of my grandmother's table,
the blackberry pie, warm with yellow butter,
set like a trophy between us.

No, this indelible remembering,
like the print of purple wine upon my girl-palms,
was the field that my grandmother had crossed,
squarely beneath the sign—
as wide and clear as the kitchen window:
　"Beware of the Bull!"
It was that she buckled on her coveralls,
thrust a dried stick of a leg over the line of fence wire,
angled her faded hair and length of old back,
between the steel-horned barbs,
silver and unyielding, like her bucket,
crossed over the field,
tangled through the thorny canes,

reached out her hand
and claimed the waiting fruit.
And it is now, in my own final years,
this taste of blackberry grit,
I wish to harvest in my woman's mouth.

Changing of the Guard

Wipers sweep arcs across the windshield.
The airport runway will have to be cleared, too, I think.
The car swerves.
Joshua corrects the slide, his hand, confident on the wheel.
Joshua means "safety." I see him in yesterday's snow,
pulling on the little boots to wade the drifts.
"Gotta feed Midnight," the small rabbit waits
in its burrowed hutch.

Joshua's middle name, Caleb: "loyal protector."
Again, the car fishtails. I voice concern. "I drive these
streets all winter, Mom." The car, our own kind of
private burrow—my son and I—against the storm.
Joshua Caleb Daniel—three Hebrew men, of whom
there is no recorded sin—though, of course, they sinned.
The first two names chosen
by his father and me. The last one inherited, like life,
like this swirling storm—lovely, threatening.

All the Bible stories I served up—in faithful bowls.
All the years of Christian school. But his father and I
swerved, fish-tailed like the car.
I ask the question mothers feel entitled:
"Has your faith survived? Philosophies? Realities?

He turns his face to mine, "Know what will drop
   you to your knees?
Wrench a prayer up from your gut? A monitor,
   threatening to
flatline. Your child dying from the cord around
   its neck."

My own breath threatens: "What did you pray?"
"Her guardian angel would breathe for her."
His words hang holy between us. And the story tells
itself all around: the swirling snow like angel's gowns,
the wipers sweeping wings across the glass.
   The baby, whose tiny globes
of lung filled with angel's breath, till she could
   breathe her own. Breath
and faith passed down and down, like angels
   changing of the guard.
And soon, I'll fly away. My son, the man of courage,
   will steer on.

Confirmation in the Laundry Room

A simplistic formula, a nearly childish drawing,
though she was not a child.
The word "God," written on one side of a chasm
a stick figure on the opposite side,
and a bridge drawn between.
"Which side are you on?" came her question.
I didn't presume to be standing on God's side,
nor was I against Him. "I'm in the middle
of the bridge," I said. "No." She was
firm in her formula. "One side or the other."
(Her creed didn't allow for process.)
I was done with her inquisition.
"I have laundry to do," I said, meaning
"I want to maintain my distance."

I filled the washer with water and soap.
I was angry, then offended. Back and forth,
in rhythm with the washer's agitation.
Why bother with such a naïve reduction
of God? But, unmistakably, the weight
of God had entered my laundry room,
heavy as the old, anchored washer.
I want to maintain my distance. . .from God?
The question sank into my *heart's chasm.*
There would be costs. And there was my pride.

Cornered in the laundry room—comic irony.
(John the Baptist would have loved
the metaphor.) The question, spinning
round and round with the cycle:
surrender or lie, surrender or lie—
not to the figment of the drawing, or
even to erudite theologies—but to God.
On my knees, surrounded by soiled socks
    and underwear,
awash with cleansing of tears, came a sweet
    knowing:
"You came over to my side, God,
    to find me here, hiding in my laundry room."

Burnt by Branta*

I sat down on the bench
close to the water's edge.
A sudden flock of geese
gathered about my knees.
Excited cackles chorused
a geese-hello.
Feathered rows, burnt-brown on grey,
their boat-shaped bodies swayed
on three-toed rubber feet.
The moment nearly magic,
a thing of fairy tales,
to suppose that creatures
can perceive and welcome
only those of trusted heart.

My vainglory was short-lived.
A woman soon arrived with her
little bag of oats and every
quill and plume of magic fled
to circle round her feet.

"I come here every day," she said.
"I try to feed the ducks," she
pointed to the Mallards
now joining in the fray.

Bobbing beaks all bit and fought
for every bite of sprinkled oats.

The woman, ducks, and geese gone,
I smiled at my shallow dupe,
mistaken for a bag of oats.
Yet, the geese did not deceive;
I fashioned ego into myth.

Jesus knew of human ways,
gathered round him on the hill.
They hadn't come for him, he said,
"They came only for the bread."

**Branta "Burnt goose,"* the old Norse name for Canadian geese, due to the burnt color of their feathers.

Earliest Light

The room where we sit is filled
with the dawn on my momma's face.
The cane chair beneath me,
gives no press against my girl legs.
Feed-sack curtains, riding
on the morning breeze, give no caress
to my memory.
The tablecloth, like my nightgown, forgets its color.
There's no fragrance from the biscuits,
still warm on the oven door.
The swallows sing in silence in the window.
My three-year-old remembering is blinded
by the blaze of one clear knowing:

I have my momma
all to myself,
and I am
a child cup
held up
to the light of her pleasure in me.

The Cipher Tree

It was a tortured day,
and Nic—so small, so scared,
the boundary of escape
beyond his vision.
Yet, as boundaries can be doors,
Nic—child-soul wide with need,
looked up to see God, sitting in a tree.
This gift to him...
God's cipher in the tree.

Early transcendent vision,
leaves its wound for life,
perhaps all pursued simulacrum,
is but the longing ache to see, once more
God in a tree.

On *our* tortured day,
we reached the boundary of our knowing,
beyond we could not see.
We nine gathered to pray, and so were ten.
Nic! Please, something for Nic!"

And as a mother strains taunt
to bear downward and birth a child to earth,
We now strain upward, stretched fierce with prayer
to birth Nic anew, beyond...beyond.

And there above Nic's body,
a crucifix,
not asked for, not planned,
God's cipher come full circle
for all of us, soul-wide with need,
this gift of God, hanging on a tree.

When

When we were children
we had no disdain
for flowers wild in the field
or blooms along the ditch rows.
They were far more wonderous
than the ordinaries in pots
our mothers watered
on the window sills,
for they were ours,
waiting treasures,
free for the find,
like ripe berries
and toads or turtles,
like puddles or creeks
and summer days,
or games of play,
released from rules
of dubious adults.
We were not yet Marthas grown
worried and troubled
about many things.
The world was free to be,
and we its seeds upon the wind.

"Aaron shall finish making atonement in the holy place, the tabernacle of testimony and the altar . . . . then he shall bring a living goat. Aaron shall place his hands on the head of the living goat, confess over it all the transgressions of the children of Israel, and all their lawlessness, and all their sins; and he shall put them on the head of the living goat and send it away into the desert. . . The goat shall bear on itself all their wrongdoings to an uninhabited land." —Leviticus 17:21-22

I've Gone Hunting for My Goat

I've gone to the desert
to look for my goat,
against all reason
as his purpose was
never to be seen again.

But here I am,
inhabiting a land,
uninhabitable.
(One cannot live here too long.)

The wilderness paths
are worn patina smooth,
trod mostly in the darkest night,
but shame can lift one's heel along
in the broadest bright of light.

Fear, failure, and lie
of worthlessness
can stride, determined, there,
against the fiercest climbs.

There is no sneaking up
upon a goat—it sees
with wild and slitted eyes,
a horizontal range, ten times
magnified—to pin me down
with clove of cutting hoof.

Once pursued,
this wasteland-scape,
can return at will:
charging in without a bell,
head-down, butting a ram
into the most absurd of
conversations—to chew my
sins, like flags in celebration!

But, a far greater One is here,
and a far greater sacrilege.
Dare I journey to the cross,
to probe the blood found there,
to thus extract my sins,
reclaim them and exempt redemption!

One drops into this
forbidden abyss
following forbidden lure.
Recon, then, the sentence:
A sin, once forgiven, is a
scene unlawful to be seen,
so, take it wholly by
the horns and herd it
till it can be heard no more.

Scarlet Manna

A hinge-turn of heaven's door
sent a thin Shekhinah ray,
through thick sky of gray,
and with it came the bird,
and with the bird came the song,
(but not its own),
and with the bird,
(now feeding in the sunlight),
came the woman,
(inside, with her phone to film the bird),
and with the filming,
came the movie, with its soundtrack,
and with the soundtrack, came the song,
and with the song, came the dead son,
who sent the manna, now recording.
Nor did she know—until
her tap upon the phone,
retrieving the Cardinal image,
brought along the manna of the song,
to leave her trembled, as though the bird
 slid open the window and stepped in to say,
"Mom—have a song I'd like you to hear. . ."

Beloved,

I come to you in the evening's shadow.
Your presence pours oil
edge to edge, across
my troubled sea-heart,
now smooth as the mirror that reflects your light.
I trace your presence
as tears trace the grateful
curve of my cheek.

For Larry

He sat outside at a small, round table,
circled by the papers of his students,
further circled by life—
his mother and his sister planting
seedlings in raised gardens,
his grandmother watching from her chair,
spinning a prayer wheel in her heart:
*that he would find a small sweetness
growing within his rounds of loss.*

Seizures had cost him college football,
his driver's license, his freedom.
And his gaze let go of expectations.
Yet, autism stored his history degree
with impeccable recall.

The mother and sister add earthworms.
Hand-grown. "Raised on table scraps,"
they tell the grandmother. "Enrich the soil."
Mothering worms, mothering their own
classrooms. Mothering him through difficult
times. Nursing seizures demanding a
backbone, unimagined for earthworms.
Seizures so cruel, they'd seen his father cry.

The nurses, now elbow deep in the
womb of soil, planting hope of harvest,
like he sought from the cycle of history.

The grandmother curious of the
papers, asks of the assignment.
"A system of government versus
the benefit of natural resources," he says,
"Which would yield the greater success?"
She nods. It's a worthy question.

His frown at each examined paper
judges each a famine of return.
Then:
"Listen to this!" he calls out.
The mother and sister hold plants mid-air.
The grandmother, still as the orb of sunlight,
shinning its halo on plants and papers.

A student has gleaned all his scattered seeds!
He holds the paper like a laurel wreath,
reading aloud, sentence after sentence,
word after word—a rich, concise yield,
and his voice sounds like pride,
like the ring of purpose.

Circumcision of the Heart

And darkness covered the face of the deep ...
and God said, "Let there be light." —Genesis 1:2-3

Out of the darkness of the womb
we are born,
as foliage births from dark of earth
in search of light.

We are temples born
with soul and spirit
sealed within,
never seen by others' eyes,
and only dimly by our own.

Light, as light must,
seeks every door;
streams on shining rays
to lightless orbs of eye,
to strike its farthest wall.

Words curl dark spirals of the ear,
tumble and change
and rearrange
in the veiled vault of the mind.

We touch and taste and live
the fragrance of the world:
its love and loss,
hope and shame,
rapture and pain,
they secret themselves within
the deepest hidden safe,
and darkness covers the face.

There is a Holy Light
whose power alone can enter in,
but the heart of the temple must be cut,
from nave to apse,
and upward soar
to pinnacles of vaulted dome,
till the inmost chamber
fills with Light,
birthing all things
inward, outward,
 new of sight.

The Eternal Mystery

The mystery,
hidden from the beginning,
inklings whisper
small prisms of light:
A star shall come forth.
A scepter shall rise.

Trickles of light gather
to hum the promise:
One is coming
It is written of Him in the scrolls.

Flashes spill rivulets of voices:
In the land of deep darkness
a light has shown.
A son of the Highest is Coming.

Sudden spills, pool whole portents:
And the government shall be upon his shoulder.
His name shall be called Wonderful,
Counselor, The Mighty God, The Everlasting Father,
The Prince of Peace.

At last, in the fullness of time,
the streams gather to a
pinnacle of clear and shining splendor,
An angel bathed in glory declares:
Behold, I bring you good tidings
of great joy which will be to all people.

The oceans of heaven open to
pour forth rejoicing:
Glory to God in the highest,
on earth, peace and good will

The radiance fills the earth's
field of night, and the shepherds
receive the first invitation,
for it is the unpretentious who understand:
Let us go and see this thing which has come to pass.

By a singular brilliance
the promise is unveiled.
There will be opulent palaces,
robes of splendor.
There will be power!

No, the promise revealed
is the shape of love,
the shape of greatest risk.
And love is ever housed in humility,
a stable of lowly creatures.
Bend the knee, and behold:
A babe, wrapped in swaddling clothes,
  lying in a manger.

The Eyes of the Heart

The eyes of the heart
receive the unseen,
as the tall grass
receives the waves of the wind.

The eyes of the heart
clear the dross, the dregs
as water clears to blue,
like truth, if truth had a color.

The eyes of the heart hear
what is wanting to be said,
and shapes the sounds
 to cry or sing the want.

The eyes of the heart
unveil the wonder of God
as raindrops reveal
rainbows hiding in the light.

www.ingramcontent.com/pod-product-compliance
Lightning Source LLC
Chambersburg PA
CBHW031301290426
44109CB00012B/674